BLACKBIRDS & LINEN

Blackbirds & Linen

Poetry for Peace

Terry-Lynn Johnson

Waterside Productions

Copyright © 2025 by Terry-Lynn Johnson
www.lakeheadpoet.com

All rights reserved. This book or any portion thereof may not be reproduced or used in any manner whatsoever without the express written permission of the publisher except for the use of brief quotations in articles and book reviews.

NO AI TRAINING: Without in any way limiting the author's [and publisher's] exclusive rights under copyright, any use of this publication to "train" generative artificial intelligence (AI) technologies to generate text is expressly prohibited. The author reserves all rights to license uses of this work for generative AI training and development of machine learning language models.

First Printing, 2025

ISBN-13: 978-1-962984-75-1 hardcover edition
ISBN-13: 978-1-962984-88-1 paperback edition
ISBN-13: 978-1-962984-89-8 ebook edition

Waterside Productions
2055 Oxford Ave
Cardiff, CA 92007
www.waterside.com

DEDICATION

*To those who seek truth and beauty
And shine with light as a beacon of hope
This book is for you.*

Table of Contents

Acknowledgement · xi
Foreword · xiii
Preface · xv
With a Note for My Children · xvii

Spring Rain · 1
    Mountainside Mist · 3
    Silent Prayer · 4
    Morning Solitude · 5
    On Your Way Home · 6
    Nest on the Windowsill · 7
    Sunday Visit · 8
    Spring Song · 9
    Clover Leaflets · 10
    Rain Boots · 11
    Morning Greeting · 12
    Lilac Boulevard in Late Spring · 13
    Lakeside Trail · 14
    Nesting Swallows · 15
    The Old Fisherman · 16
    Boardwalk Railings · 17
    Moments of Grace · 18
    Morning Mist · 19

- Summer Days · 21
  - Beacon Hill Park · 23
  - Serenity of Moments · 24
  - Conch Shells and Sunrise · 25
  - Beacon · 26
  - Faith · 27
  - Sands of Time · 28
  - Wildflower Petals · 29
  - Guardian Angels · 30
  - Field Clover · 31
  - Bicycle Parade · 32
  - Backwoods Grove · 33
  - Blackbird's Keynote · 34
  - Soil of Compassion · 35
  - Blackbirds and Linen · 36
  - Grandmother's Apron · 37
  - Small Blessings · 38
  - The Flower Box · 39
  - Braided Daisies · 40
  - Campfire Songs · 41
  - Good Poetry · 42
  - Poetry on a Summer Day · 43
  - The Old Farmhouse · 44
  - The Urban Crow · 45
  - Blackbird's Song · 46
  - Songbird on the Fence · 47
  - Roses and Berries · 48
  - Field Flowers and Ribbon · 49
  - Teacup Kintsugi · 50
  - Sit With the Day · 51
  - By the Birdfeeder · 52
  - Simple Blessings · 53
  - Summer Rain · 54
  - Blackbird in the Rain · 55
  - Wilted Rose Bushes · 56

Corner Piece · 57
Vintage Cribbage · 58
Last Goodbyes · 59
Bedside Visit · 60
Nature Trail · 61
Morning on the Lake · 62
By the Wayside · 63

Fall Colours · 65
   Man in The Moon · 67
   The Old Country · 68
   Fall Comforts · 69
   Country Church · 70
   Rustic Beauty · 71
   Golden Woods · 72
   Warm Coffee · 73
   Coffee Shop Date · 74
   Pumpkin Spice Coffee · 75
   Fall Sweater · 76
   Fall Apple Tree · 77

Winter Songs · 79
   Bohemian Waxwings · 81
   Cherry Wood Door · 82
   Post-It Note · 83
   Frost Moon · 84
   Mourning Dove · 85
   Winter Starlight · 86
   Morning Flurries · 87
   Winter Mist · 88
   Mid-January Freeze · 89
   Winter Songbird · 90
   Peace on the Wayside · 91
   Morning Hours · 92
   Season To Heal · 93

Valentine Roses	94
A Sunday Morning in March	95
Brushed Winter Buds	96
Thermal Cup	97
Perennial Notes	99
Peace At Home	101
Spare Time	102
On Love	103
Stitches of Love	104
Life's Lessons	105
Journal Page	106
Stay True	107
Blueprint of Life	108
Soar With Hope	109
Season of Compassion	110
Morning Star	111
Embrace Peace	112
For the Moment	113
Dust Off the Stars	114
Follow Your Daydreams	115
Find Your Way	116
You Are Enough	117
Shine For the Day	118
Swinging on a Star	119
Index of Opening Phrases	121
About the Author	125
Index of Re-Published Poems	127

Acknowledgement

To My Mentors

You are cherished as we travel down the road together.

Foreword

In a world that often feels weird, sometimes crazy and many times overwhelming, *Blackbirds & Linen: Poetry for Peace* emerges as a sanctuary for the soul.

Terry-Lynn's poetry invites readers to pause, reflect, and reconnect with the delicate beauty of life, nature, and our shared human experiences. With each turn of the page, we are swept into a realm where the ordinary transforms into the extraordinary and where moments of grace and whispers of hope are captured in the essence of poetic art.

The collection is a tapestry woven from the threads of nature, love, and introspection. The titles—ranging from "Mountainside Mist" to "Swinging on a Star"—evoke imagery that is both familiar and enchanting. Each poem serves as a guiding light, illuminating the paths of our hearts and minds with a gentle touch. Whether it's the serene "Morning Solitude" or the nostalgic "Grandmother's Apron," Terry-Lynn's words resonate deeply, reminding us of the beauty that lies in both the mundane and the profound.

In *Blackbirds & Linen*, we encounter a celebration of life's seasons. From the vibrant blooms of spring to the quiet introspection of winter, the poetry reflects the cyclical nature of existence. Terry-Lynn has an extraordinary ability to capture fleeting moments—from pure joy as a child offers the timid bird "millet and seed with outstretched hand on the trail" ("Nature Trail" lines 6-8) to a tender and poignant Sunday visit when "the moment is passed for goodbyes" and "a tear on your cheek" is "wiped with the brush of an angel." ("Sunday Visit" lines 7-11). The verses in *Blackbirds and Linen* mirror our own joys and sorrows, reminding us that we are never truly alone in our experience.

This collection is not only a testament to Terry-Lynn's artistic talent but also a call to embrace peace and compassion in our lives. In today's tumultuous world, her poetry resonates with a message of healing and understanding. It beckons us to find solace in nature, to nurture our relationships, and to cultivate a spirit of gratitude. Each poem is an invitation to pause and reflect, to immerse ourselves in the present moment, and to find beauty in the everyday.

As you journey through these pages, I encourage you to savor the words, allowing them to wash over you like a gentle breeze. Let the imagery and emotions evoke memories and inspire new thoughts. *Blackbirds & Linen: Poetry for Peace* is not just a collection of poems; it is an experience—a reminder that amidst life's complexities, we can always return to the simple yet profound beauty that surrounds us.

May you find peace within these words, and may they inspire you to embrace the beauty of your own journey.

With warm regards,

Live a Courageous Life

Ken D Foster

Preface

> *"Joy and woe are woven fine,*
> *A clothing for the soul divine"*
> William Blake

I am pleased to share with you my new collection of poetry *Blackbirds & Linen: Poetry for Peace* with foreword by Ken D. Foster, Voices of Courage.us. The nature and life poetry in this collection reflects on what is common to human experience and the blackbird motif adds a sense of delight to the collection.

My love for poetry was instilled in me by my grandfather when I was young and my first poems were published with a mimeograph by my middle grade teacher. It is of interest to me as to how many copies are still around of this chapbook. There are a few gems of my first poems republished in S*prigs and Twigs: A Solitary Note & Selected Poems, Collector's Edition* (2021).

The poetry in *Blackbirds & Linen* is arranged by subject, tone and season and all of the poems in this collection have been written since publication of *Driftwood Tones: Nature Poetry of Beauty & Presence* (2023).

You will find the poetry in *Blackbirds & Linen* as comfortable as the old, soft and faded blue jeans that you pull from your drawer for those quiet and relaxing days. Overall tones of harmony and peace will be your companion as you curl up with this collection. May there be peace in your corner of the world.

Poetry is for you.

With warm regards,

Terry-Lynn Johnson
Canadian Poet and Educator

With a Note for My Children

You travel your own road with grace and fortitude
And I am writing this note to let you know
how much you mean to me
And how my love is unconditional
for you.

Spring Rain

Spring rain brings songs
of solitude and hope

@lakeheadpoet

Mountainside Mist

With robe and
sandals in
morning mist
My soul yearns
to touch the hem
of the garment.
And as mist rises
I walk with
serenity.

Silent Prayer

Your silent petition
is the most earnest
of prayer
Stillness knowing the
promise of compassion
With hands outstretched
in the heavenly mist
on the hillside.
Be at peace
Christ is with
you.

Morning Solitude

The early hours
of morning
bring a sense of
contentment
With fragrant hues
of lilacs
in heavenly mist.
The sparrow's call
beckoning grace
with morning
solitude.

On Your Way Home

The spring blossoms
are scented with
memories of you—
And you're on your
way home.

Nest on the Windowsill

The empty nest sits
on the garden shed
windowsill
The wrens darting about
the grounds before leaving
for winter.
Spring returns with
fledglings on the sill
And wrens flitting about
golden daffodils
The garden shed
weathered with
season.

Sunday Visit

The bird feeder
is empty outside
your window
You frail and the
mushroom soup
cold.
A tear on your cheek
wiped with the brush
of an angel.
The moment passed
for goodbyes.

Spring Song

Blue notes
in the morning mist
promise rain
And you will not always
wake to sunshine
As both rain and shine
enrich the greens
of June.

CLOVER LEAFLETS

The child props on
elbows in the field
looking for a
four leaflet clover—
And the clover
is pressed between
the pages of life
with innocence.

Rain Boots

Spring brings us back
to the delight of
childhood sail—
with a leaf or twig
placed in the runoff
of melting snow.
The sail travels under
ridges of ice,
through culverts,
and along banks.
And birds return with
spring song and
splash of rain
boots.

Morning Greeting

My friend the crow
greets me
with syllabic notes
in the light spring rain
And I could not help but
be delighted
With the antics of this
songbird—
Having no concern other
than my whereabouts
and business
Before taking flight,
as crows fly,
into the day.

Lilac Boulevard in Late Spring

The June rain falls
on the wet pavement
As I walk by your house
The windows empty
and boxes by the
curbside.
Walking down the street
in late spring rain
With thoughts of you.
The lilac shrubs tarnished
on the boulevard.

Lakeside Trail

The mossy bedded path
through the woods leads
me home
The old boat moored
as nature's planter
With tall birches and shrubs
through the rusty hull.
You will find the frame
of the old rusted boat
and bird feeders
Along the mossy path
of the lakeside trail.

Nesting Swallows

The swallows dart
to and fro
feeding young
Carving the sky
in agile flight.
The nestlings chirp
from hollow nests
built in the rafters
of parkland shelter
With marshland
browns golden in
morning sun.

The Old Fisherman

The painted wood rowboat
sits on the shore in morning fog
As the loon call echoes
and water lilies sway
just beyond the shallow
of the shoreline.
The fog lifts and
the old fisherman
sits on the morning lake—
the still surface of the water
reflecting the painted
wood rowboat.

Boardwalk Railings

The tangled strands
of web sparkle with
droplets of morning
rain—
Spun in the corners
of boardwalk railings
with the strength
of hope.

Moments of Grace

Grace bathes you with light
and forgiveness
As you kneel by the glacier stream
which feeds the river.
Grateful for the crystal clear water.
The stream tumbles with poetry
over bedrock and pebbles
to the valley—
And you rest by the stream
with grace.

Morning Mist

Peace weeps with
morning rain
And tears refresh the soil
as skies lift with morning light.
The finch chirps sweetly in
morning mist
With no concern as to the day
but to pass the hour.
Peace weeps with
morning rain.

S<small>UMMER</small> D<small>AYS</small>

Summer days bring the blackbird's
note of reflection
@lakeheadpoet

Beacon Hill Park

My God is hidden
from me—
Yet I know of love,
compassion,
grief and sorrow
And delight as the sun
rises behind the branches
of the weeping willow
With painted turtles basking
on the log.
We stroll along the riverside
on a carpet of green grass,
and talk about little things.
My soul is grateful for the day
and for the time spent
with you—
Under the morning sun
by the riverside.

Serenity of Moments

The morning breeze rustles
the leaves with exaltation
And tranquility stays with you
for the day—
As once you hear the lift of praise
you cannot miss it.
Peace is a simple gift found in
the serenity of moments.

Conch Shells and Sunrise

There's a sense of wonder
when the conch shell is held
to a child's ear
With the lull of the ocean
and corals of sunrise.
Days are busy with
human affairs—
Yet a moment with beauty
is as wide and deep as
the ocean's call
And needs no purpose
with its sublimity.

Beacon

Set your compass
with intention
of compassion
As a beacon
of peace.

Faith

Faith is courage
to rise
as rays of sun
break over your shoulder
And waves crest
the shoreline.

Sands of Time

Know the unity
of compassion
with joy and sorrow
And the essence
of what it is to be
infinitely human
As the sun sets
over the beach sands.

Wildflower Petals

Your days are like
wildflowers
As you hike the terrain
of the loop trail
With petals strewn
along the bedded path.
And it is to Him
the trail returns.

Guardian Angels

Angels protect me.
I see them in flight
As they light up my world.
Angels guide me.
I see them sitting in trees
on branches, with fancy—
As even angels
need rest.

Field Clover

The honeybee pollinates the field
of clover.
Collecting nectar with brief summer days
And what you have started may not be
for your lifetime—
As it is not of worth in gold
but of sweetness at the
end of the day.

Bicycle Parade

My trike was painted
red
And with tissue flowers
on handlebars
I entered the parade
To learn,
new is better, even
then.
And tissue flowers
are not for the rain.

Backwoods Grove

You know the note of each
songbird on the backwoods trail
With the white-throated sparrow's call
and the robust chatter of
pine siskins
hidden in a canopy of green—
The sunlight dappling the forest floor.
Rest at His feet with moment
of divine solitude
in the field beside the woods
As the old hymn lifts in
morning mist
over the wildflowers.

Blackbird's Keynote

The blackbird hits a keynote
of complaint
And our hearts will not
be turned from grief
With the blackbird's
supplication
over morning hours.

Soil of Compassion

The small bird hidden
in branch
chirps tenderly
And cumulus clouds
rest over the hill
Where the road meets
the heavens.
The morning sun
breaks through with
streams of glory—
And my soul weeps
with the sweet chirp—
The world needs love
grounded in the soil
of compassion.

Blackbirds and Linen

We shelled sweet peas
from the kitchen garden
With blackbirds and linen
on the clothesline—
Fly pretty blackbirds.
The rain barrel is empty.
The odd clothespin on line
with lavender skies
and wheat fields—
Greet us after the rain
with your song.

Grandmother's Apron

I enjoyed the comfort
of creamed peas
on toast at the farmhouse
kitchen table.
Grandma wiped her hands
on her apron—
Content with the busyness
of farmhouse chores.
Days were simple
and summer short.

Small Blessings

Florets adorn the green fields
With evening dew on rays of white.
The morning breaks with
early light—
The bird song clear
with notes of harmony.

The Flower Box

I spent my day with pollinating
bees in the flower box.
And with the day passing by
All ends well.
Sitting for tea without you
But with the good company
of garden angels and
honeybees.

Braided Daisies

Daisies bask in fields
with evening sun
And love keeps you
young
With sandals on your feet
And daisies braided
in your hair.
Enjoying folk
And songs of
freedom.

Campfire Songs

Join me this summer's
evening—
And catch the wonder
of sitting and gazing
into the campfire
As the wood crackles
under the stars
And cricket frogs sing
in the dark.
We'll enjoy campfire songs,
roast marshmallows,
and share stories as the
evening wears on
With good company
around the campfire.

Good Poetry

I would settle for
good poetry
And be lonely
without you—
Than gain in this world
what little there is to gain.
But I would rather write
songs with a bottle
of wine
And let the world pass
on by—
As I fall in love
with you.

Poetry on a Summer Day

I am sitting on
the deck with my
morning coffee
With the book
of poems you
gifted to me
As the birds sing
of this beautiful
summer day.

The Old Farmhouse

The high note of the
blackbird's song brings me
to the old farmhouse—
As the clothesline wheel draws in
the morning's laundry
And chicks chirp under the brooding
lamp with fresh farm eggs
gathered in basket.
Perhaps nostalgia wanes as clouds
dissipate into crystal skies—
And the beauty is in the
blackbird's song.

The Urban Crow

The crow flew over
and settled in branches
Watching me with curiosity
As I walked my leashed dog
down the street—
Cawing with content
on the misty morning.
I was curious as to his interest
in my presence with his sharp eye
and silhouette in the branches.
And I fancied it is only me
that notices such things
As I wished him a good day.
And he purred namaste
with a nodding bow.

Blackbird's Song

Trust the day
with peace of mind
And be grateful for the hour
As you know not what
the day brings
Before the golden sun
sets over the lake—
With the blackbird's
evening song.

Songbird on the Fence

You're a long way from home
With your guitar strapped over
your shoulder.
The sun rises with crimson skies
and wild clover.
The songbird sits on the fence post
with sheet notes for the day
And you rest by the country road—
A long way from home.

Roses and Berries

Red raspberries were picked
for you to sweeten your
cold cereal
As an act of kindness.
The evening's sunset over
the rose bushes.
But the picked berries
left to overripe.
I should be kind to myself
And pick fresh berries
for me
For raspberries and cream.
And a wild rose for
the vase.

Field Flowers and Ribbon

I gathered flowers
for you
As a child in the field
with a broken heart
And only now
love dried bouquets
of field flowers
tied with a
ribbon.

Teacup Kintsugi

Celebrate the lacquered
seam of the teacup
Fill it with joy.
And know that you're beautiful
And strong and fragile.
Enjoy your cup of tea
As you embrace
and mend with
self-care.

Sit With the Day

Life brings tears with
lessons, not all fair
And summer days pass
by quickly
Though I had to pause
when you said you're sorry
as I walked out the door.
Sit with the day over coffee
And then carry on and
wipe your tears.

By the Birdfeeder

Do not bring worry
to your day
Rather, sit quietly by
the bird feeder
And watch the
goldfinches
Simply yield to presence
And let God work in you
and through you—
As the golden thread
in life is the peace
of compassion.

Simple Blessings

Be happy with the simple
things in life as they turn
into the big things
An early morning walk
in diffused light with
daisies along the roadside.
French toast, cinnamon sugar
And moments over coffee
Just to name a few—
Walking in the rain
Birds at the feeder
Summer sunsets and
starlit nights—
Good friends and
family.
Start your day grateful
for the simple things in life
And your heart will open
to blessings.

Summer Rain

The smallest blessings
bring grace—
The bluebells in the field—
The morning mist after
summer rain
And the brown finch
hidden in the tall grass
with a broken wing.
Trust the day with
whatever it may bring—
As faith brings you
to grace, and peace
With comfort of
whispered truth
on the breeze.

BLACKBIRD IN THE RAIN

The blackbird
sits on the
white picket fence
Singing in the
summer rain
of fairer weather.

Wilted Rose Bushes

The rose bushes
border the yard by
the garden table
And need watering with
the summer's heat
As we share a pitcher
of ice-tea.
I know you're not
good for me—
Fare thee well, my friend—
My time is better spent
caring for the wilted
roses.

Corner Piece

The finish is worn
thin on the kitchen table
The puzzle pieces placed
over coffee and news.
The crow caws over early hours
from atop the hydro pole.
And the world settles
into daily routine—
the corner piece of
puzzle amiss.

Vintage Cribbage

We sit at the table
with our memories
playing cribbage.
And time passes fast
as we round fourth street
with double run.
You will soon leave.
And I will grieve—
and put away the
cribbage board.

Last Goodbyes

I wept at your
bedside
And later left
a rose
on the cold ground
by your graveside
For last
goodbyes.

Bedside Visit

The old man asked
"Where's your grandma?"
And grandchild
by bedside
replied—
"With you.
Rest."

Nature Trail

Be still and what
you seek will come
to you—
Like a timid bird
As the child offers
millet and seed
With outstretched hand
on the trail.

Morning on the Lake

The old fisherman sits
with shoulders bent
and rounded
And gathers his woven
net with bounty of
good catch
into his wooden boat.
The morning loon
calls from distance
as the fog rolls out
over the lake—
With water lilies
painted in the shallows
of the bay.

By the Wayside

We all know the depth
and longing of wonder—
By the camp fireside as
the water reflects tranquility
with sunset.
By the lakeside with the
quiet wake of the loon's
morning call.
And by the wayside—
When beloved hands
fold with sacred
pause.

Fall Colours

Fall colours bring amber tones
as you travel home
@lakeheadpoet

Man in the Moon

The full moon lies above
the landscape
Glowing bright with
silhouettes of pine
in the maroon skyline.
With countenance resting
over the foothills—
As you round the bend
and travel into the
new day.

The Old Country

The gentleman tosses
grains to the pigeons
in the city square—
like a scene from an
old movie.
Wrapped in his tweed coat
with his newspaper bundled
under arm.
The pigeons coo
in morning air—
The leaves bronzed with
wine and romance
of fall harvest.

Fall Comforts

The mist burns off
the emblazoned hillside
And as leaves rain
from the branches
You delight in the dance
with the beauty of fall.
Tomorrow is not promised
But for today
the season brings
fall comforts.

Country Church

The pumpkins are harvested
with frosted vines
The old country church
in field beyond with steeple
The blue morning skies
powdered with cotton white
over the stretch of road
There is something about
an old country church
on a lonely road
that brings me home.

Rustic Beauty

The blackbird sits on
the round fence post
dry with age
His feathers iridescent
with morning light.
Border trees cast dancing
shadows on the old
farmhouse road
The blackbird's note
rustic beauty
with breaking day.

Golden Woods

The journey is long
before rest
With thought as to what
you missed
What could be different
What was done well
And what needs
forgiveness.
Your honest reflection
brings you to searching
for your true self
As patches of sunlight
brighten the woods.
Share your trials, joys and
sorrows
He will answer with mercy
and grace
And will rest with you
on the golden trail
that leads you
home.

Warm Coffee

The sideways rain
brought chill to the day.
As you bought a warm
coffee for the homeless
youth on the curbside.
Acts of kindness are
remembered—
But benevolence repaid
with gratefulness
the real treasure.

Coffee Shop Date

You order coffee black
Your thoughts private
as you glance at your
phone.
Something is lost
As we left us behind
building our dreams.

Pumpkin Spice Coffee

How could you not love
September—
When the mystic daybreak
tugs at your soul.
You wrap in your oatmeal sweater
With pumpkin spice coffee
as the morning passes
slowly—
Even the bee bumbles from
clover to clover in no hurry.
The days of September
comfort an old soul—
As the season changes
to autumn.

Fall Sweater

Your sweater is on
the top shelf
And on crystal mornings
when frost is settled
on rooftops
I wrap it around my shoulders
with warmth of variegated
fall colours.
Just to be close to you.

Fall Apple Tree

The hues of low rising sun
warm the bare apple tree
Standing stoically rooted
and dormant in my
neighbour's yard.
Fall leaves and branches
are strewn about the lawn
With sleet and rain lending
a stillness to early hours.
Daylight rounds into
mid-November with its
poetry of late fall
And the comforts of
this small northern town
bring me home.

Winter Songs

Winter songs bring frosted notes
of beauty

@lakeheadpoet

Bohemian Waxwings

The warmer winter brings waxwings
to my neck of the woods
The flock carving flight in the sky
before settling on branches of ash
With tawned colours and chitter sweet
like the sprinkling of cinnamon
and berries.
Their visit brief before travelling on
under morning sun
With free lifestyle and
no worries.

Cherry Wood Door

The ice is thin on the
windowpane
With the skeleton key in the
keyhole of the cherry wood door.
The room empty but for a feather
divinely settling on a wisp of air.
You expected me to find the key
And you're now on your way
to wherever it is that
old poets rest.

Post-It Note

I found the rusted key
And picked up the feather
with baritone and shimmer
On the way back from
our journey.

Frost Moon

The frost moon
of late November
is clear in the
indigo sky.
And I am comforted
with frozen crystals
on divine wings
Tucked in with warmth
of white feathers
As I grieve for days
before winter
solstice.

Mourning Dove

The mourning dove
sits on the hydro wire
With silhouette in
crystal frost.
By the turnpike
off the two-lane
blacktop.
Bringing peace to
the frosted morning
And peace to the
weary traveller
on the road.

Winter Starlight

Wintering birds
shelter with stillness
Under mystic
starlight as you struggle
to rest—
Knowing what it is
to walk and weep
with Christ.

Morning Flurries

The sweet notes of songbirds
rise from the shelter of branch
As the wintry morning breaks
with peace.
The beauty of flurries blanketed
with bedding of soft light—
Under slate of grey
winter skies.

Winter Mist

Branches are frosted
in winter mist with
morning hours
My home quiet
but for the wall clock
ticking off increments
of time.
I may never travel
and see the world
But know of our
need for peace.
Beauty beckons peace
And is tucked into
corners of the world
with serenity.

Mid-January Freeze

I hide my age well
as I count my years—
But my bones know exactly
how old they are with the chill
of winter
As I bundle up warm to take
my dog for a walk—
Grateful for her company
And the refreshing
winter air.

Winter Songbird

We travel alone
on the road
As the winter songbird
uplifts our brokenness
with notes of beauty.
Be still with me—
And let love thaw
our trials, grief and
sorrow.
Be still with me
And embrace
the divinity of
our soul.

Peace on the Wayside

The gate is open
by the country
cemetery
With the rustic beauty
of the common grackle
and wintered twigs
along the roadside.
Beauty is the path
to peace
Yet we travel down
the road with peace
on the wayside.

Morning Hours

My soul searches
for grace with
morning hours
And settles in peace
with the stillness
of golden light.

Season To Heal

Just as winter pruning
brings new spring
growth
Your work and faith
determine today
With season
to heal.

Valentine Roses

I knew about her
when the roses sent
for Valentine's
never bloomed.
And I forgave you.
But, I never forgave
myself for losing
your love.

A Sunday Morning in March

The leaves tumble across the
snow swept yard
And your empty mug sits
on the coffee table
As a single snowflake drifts
by the windowpane.
You know not what the
day brings—
The world warm and loving
and cold and hard at once.
The crows caw
and face the wind in flight
And you greet the day—
Curled up with a book
and a fresh cup of coffee
On a Sunday morning
in March.

Brushed Winter Buds

Walk with me in the woods
brushed with winter buds
The trail with ice under shade
of pine
And we will sit on the fallen tree
by the creekside
With water high and tumbling
along frozen banks.
We'll spend some time in the
awakening woods
With season early for spring.
And perhaps,
we will find a fluted note
of contentment.

Thermal Cup

Pause with
appreciation for
another day
As you run with
coffee in your
thermal cup.
Take a moment
As the universe lends
peace to the bustle
of daily life.

Perennial Notes

Perennial notes harmonize
changing seasons

@lakeheadpoet

Peace At Home

Compassion soars
with peace
And love shelters
under divine wings
Bringing peace
home.

SPARE TIME

Seize opportunities of
good times and memories—
Extend a loving hand
Offering support and
encouragement.
Spare time but
share your company—
Life passes by quickly with
unresolved goodbyes.

On Love

Love warms your heart
and nurtures your soul.
Love sits by the window
Lights a candle
And waits for you
to find your way.
Love embraces the
stillness of patience
And cradles the beauty
of season.
Love carries forward
with timeless truth
and cherished
moments.

STITCHES OF LOVE

Children are the
fabric of a mother's soul
And are stitched into
Every moment.
The charm squares
quilted with timeless
love.

Life's Lessons

Life is not always fair
And that is just part of
living fully.
Allow sorrow to teach
you empathy—
As tomorrow there may
be one who needs you
to care.
And you know what
it is to struggle alone.

Journal Page

Time heals old hurts
but sacred tears smudge
the ink on the page
of your journal.

STAY TRUE

Greet each day with
harmony
And embrace the day
Knowing the crow
as a trickster and black line
greeting card.
Embrace the day as you
blaze your trail through field
and woods
As the best you can do
with each day is to be true
to yourself.

Blueprint of Life

When tears from heaven
smudge your blueprint
of life—
Know the divine is
seeking you.

Soar With Hope

Hope is like the
soaring eagle above
with shadow cast
in flight—
Hope against hope
with no fear in your
heart.
Hope is faith
beneath your wings.

Season of Compassion

The bee gathers
sweetness
from thistles in
midst of the field
And compassion
holds both joy
and sorrow
with each season.

Morning Star

Wish for love on the morning star
as it fades into the heavens
And believe in the joy
of your dreams.
As magic happens.

Embrace Peace

Embrace peace with
the glory of presence
And your light will shine
in the darkest
of nights.

For the Moment

Let go of your cares
And do not worry about
what others may or may not do
How they make you feel
What may or may not happen.
Appreciate your light and
let go of the rest—
Just for the moment.
As the moment parts the
deepest water between you
and peace and presence.

Dust Off the Stars

Lead your purpose
with grace
And your intention
will align your dreams.
Reach for the sky
And love will dust
off the stars.

Follow Your Daydreams

Build castles in the sky
and follow your
daydreams—
Your radiance shines
with your brand
of resilience.

Find Your Way

Find your way as you
walk in the light
of change
As it is never too late
to make a difference
in our world.

You Are Enough

Dreams are hindered
with practicalities
And not for
everyone.
Find joy in your life
And you will be the
light of your essence.

Shine For the Day

Shine for the day
With stardust in your hair
And glitter in your soul.
Be bright, be humble.
Commit your best
Knowing you do not need
to be the best.
Know your gifts are
blessings.
Stand proud with delight—
not pride.
Know life brings rain
and shine
And be grateful
for the day.

Swinging on a Star

Start your day
with peace, beauty
and song.
And here, you will
be grateful.
Your worry will not
change the world.
But your light brings
hope for good.
And, it's delightful
swinging on
a star.

Index of Opening Phrases

Angels protect me (30)
Be happy with the simple things in life as they
 turn into the big things (53)
Be still and what you seek will come to you (61)
Blue notes in the morning mist promise rain (9)
Branches are frosted in winter mist with morning hours (88)
Build castles in the sky and follow your daydreams (115)
Celebrate the lacquered seam of the teacup (50)
Children are the fabric of a mother's soul (104)
Compassion soars with peace (101)
Daisies bask in fields with evening sun (40)
Do not bring worry to your day (52)
Dreams are hindered with practicalities (117)
Embrace peace with the glory of presence (112)
Faith is courage to rise (27)
Find your way as you walk in the light of change (116)
Florets adorn the green fields with evening dew on rays of white (38)
Grace bathes you with light and forgiveness (18)
Greet each day with harmony (107)
Hope is like the soaring eagle above with shadow cast in flight (109)
How could you not love September when the mystic daybreak
 tugs at your soul (75)
I am sitting on the deck with my morning coffee (43)

I enjoyed the comfort of creamed peas on toast
   at the farmhouse kitchen table (37)
I found the rusted key (83)
I gathered flowers for you (49)
I hide my age well as I count my years (89)
I knew about her when the roses sent for Valentine's never bloomed (94)
I spent my day with pollinating bees in the flower box (39)
I wept at your bedside (59)
I would settle for good poetry and be lonely without you (42)
Join me this summer's evening and catch the wonder of sitting
   and gazing into the campfire (41)
Just as winter pruning brings new spring growth (93)
Know the unity of compassion with joy and sorrow (28)
Lead your purpose with grace (114)
Let go of your cares (113)
Life brings tears with lessons, not all fair (51)
Life is not always fair and that is just part of living fully (105)
Love warms your heart and nurtures your soul (103)
My friend the crow greets me with syllabic notes in the
   light spring rain (12)
My God is hidden from me (23)
My soul searches for grace with morning hours (92)
My trike was painted red (32)
Pause with appreciation for another day (97)
Peace weeps with morning rain (19)
Red raspberries were picked for you to sweeten your cold cereal (48)
Seize opportunities of good times and memories (102)
Set your compass with intention of compassion (26)
Shine for the day with stardust in your hair and glitter
   in your soul (118)
Spring brings us back to the delight of childhood sail (11)
Start your day with peace, beauty and song (119)
The bee gathers sweetness from thistles in midst of the field (110)
The bird feeder is empty outside of your window (8)

The blackbird hits a keynote of complaint (34)
The blackbird sits on the round fence post dry with age (71)
The blackbird sits on the white picket fence (55)
The child props on elbows in the field looking
    for a four leaflet clover (10)
The crow flew over and settled in branches (45)
The early hours of morning bring a sense of contentment (5)
The empty nest sits on the garden shed windowsill (7)
The finish is worn thin on the kitchen table (57)
The frost moon of late November is clear in the indigo sky (84)
The full moon lies above the landscape (67)
The gate is open by the country cemetery (91)
The gentleman tosses grains to the pigeons in the city square (68)
The high note of the blackbird's song brings me to the
    old farmhouse (44)
The honeybee pollinates the field of clover (31)
The hues of low rising sun warm the bare apple tree (77)
The ice is thin on the windowpane (82)
The journey is long before rest (72)
The June rain falls on the wet pavement (13)
The leaves tumble across the snow swept yard (95)
The mist burns off the emblazoned hillside (69)
The morning breeze rustles the leaves with exaltation (24)
The mossy bedded path through the woods leads me home (14)
The mourning dove sits on the hydro wire (85)
The old fisherman sits with shoulders bent and rounded (62)
The old man asked "Where's your grandma?" (60)
The painted wood rowboat sits on the shore in morning fog (16)
The pumpkins are harvested with frosted vines (70)
The rose bushes border the yard by the garden table (56)
The sideways rain brought chill to the day (73)
The small bird hidden in branch chirps tenderly (35)
The smallest blessings bring grace (54)
The spring blossoms are scented with memories of you (6)

The swallows dart to and fro feeding young (15)
The sweet notes of the songbirds rise from shelter of branch (87)
The tangled strands of web sparkle with droplets
    of morning rain (17)
The warmer winter brings waxwings to my neck of the woods (81)
There is a sense of wonder when the conch
    shell is held to a child's ear (25)
Time heals old hurts (106)
Trust the day with peace of mind (46)
Walk with me in the woods brushed with winter buds (96)
We all know the depth and longing of wonder (63)
We shelled sweet peas from the kitchen garden (36)
We sit at the table with our memories playing cribbage (58)
When tears from heaven smudge your blueprint of life (108)
We travel alone on the road (90)
Wintering birds shelter with stillness (86)
Wish for love on the morning star (111)
With robe and sandals in morning mist (3)
You know the note of each songbird on the backwoods trail (33)
You order coffee black (74)
Your days are like wildflowers (29)
Your silent petition is the most earnest of prayer (4)
Your sweater is on the top shelf (76)
You're a long way from home (47)

About the Author

Canadian poet Terry-Lynn Johnson was born in Nipigon, Ontario. Her modern romantic poetry has themes of nature, spirituality, beauty and presence with reflection on what is common to human experience. She is a graduate of Lakehead University with an Honours in English and Master of Education.

Previous publications include *This Christmas: Seasonal Poems for Peace* (2024) with foreword by Ken D. Foster, Voices of Courage, *Driftwood Tones: Nature Poetry of Beauty & Presence* (2023) with foreword by Philip V. Allingham, Ph.D., Professor Emeritus, Formerly: Faculty of Education, and Adjunct Professor, Department of English, Lakehead University and *Sprigs and Twigs: A Solitary Note & Selected Poems* (2021). *Blackbirds & Linen: Poetry for Peace* is poetry written after the spring publication of *Driftwood Tones: Nature Poetry of Beauty & Presence* (2023).

She enjoys Romantic, Victorian and modernist poetry. Her grandfather introduced her to Robert Frost's poetry and the Romantics at a young age and she started writing poetry at the age of twelve after the passing of her mother. Favourite poets include Leonard Cohen, Maya Angelou and her Canadian contemporary Atticus.

Her husband Michael Kivari is a professional recording artist and together they perform acoustic music and poetry at a variety of venues along the scenic northwestern shores of Lake Superior.

INDEX OF RE-PUBLISHED POEMS

from *This Christmas Seasonal Poems for Peace*
Waterside Productions, 2024

Winter Starlight
Morning Flurries

www.ingramcontent.com/pod-product-compliance
Lightning Source LLC
LaVergne TN
LVHW020933090426
835512LV00020B/3334